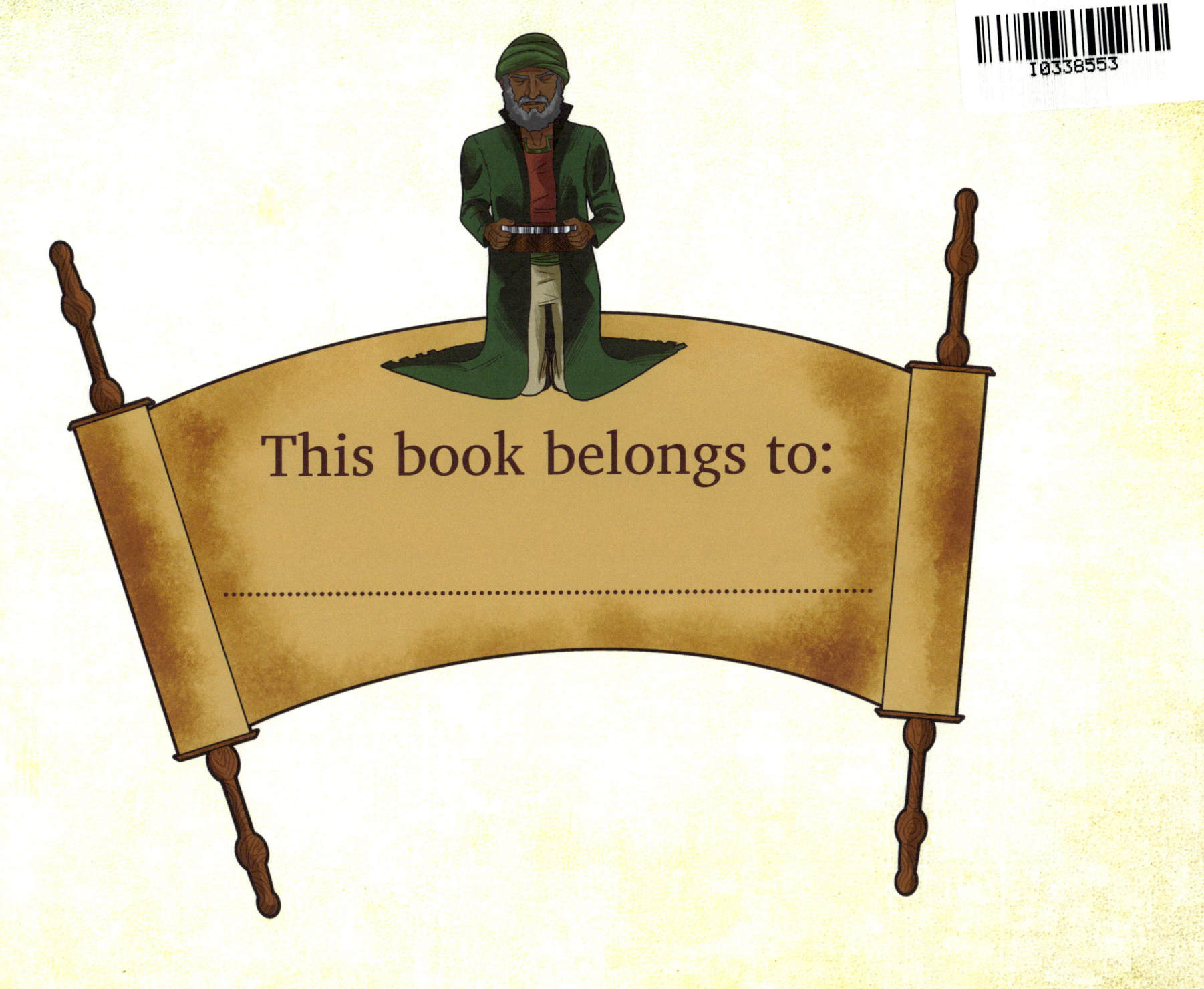

This book belongs to:

....

Copyright © BPA Publishing Ltd 2020

Author: Pip Reid
Illustrator: Thomas Barnett
Creative Director: Curtis Reid

www.biblepathwayadventures.com

Thank you for supporting Bible Pathway Adventures®. Our adventure series helps parents teach their children more about the Bible in a fun creative way. Designed for the whole family, Bible Pathway Adventures' mission is to help bring discipleship back into homes around the world. The search for truth is more fun than tradition!

The moral rights of author and illustrator have been asserted, this book is copyright.

ISBN: 978-0-473-41744-4

Birth of The King

The Messiah is born!

"Where is He that is born King of the Jews? For we have seen His star from the east, and have come to worship Him." (Matthew 2:2)

One cold winter's night in Nazareth, a young Hebrew woman named Mary sat by the fire, warming her feet. Suddenly, an angel of God appeared in the doorway. Mary looked up and gasped. "Who are you?" she cried. She had never seen an angel before.

"Don't be afraid," said the angel, whose name was Gabriel. "God is happy with you. You have been chosen to have a baby boy. You will call Him Yeshua and He will be the Son of the Most High."

"How can I have a baby?" asked Mary. "I'm not married yet." The angel looked at Mary and smiled. "God will send His Holy Spirit to give you this baby." Mary stared at the angel, wide-eyed. She was more puzzled than ever. "Remember your cousin Elizabeth?" continued Gabriel. "Everyone knew she couldn't have children, but now she's six months pregnant. With God, nothing is impossible!"

Early the next morning Mary jumped out of bed and hurried to see her fiancé, Joseph. *"How will I tell him I'm going to have a baby?"* she wondered. She tiptoed along the narrow alleyway to Joseph's home.

Taking a deep breath, Mary pushed open the door. "Joseph, Joseph," she whispered, "an angel called Gabriel came to see me. He said not to be afraid. God has given us a baby!"

Joseph's eyes flew open. An angel had visited Mary? She was going to have a baby? He gulped nervously and scrambled down the wooden ladder from his bed. "But Mary, we're not married yet," he said. "How could this happen?"

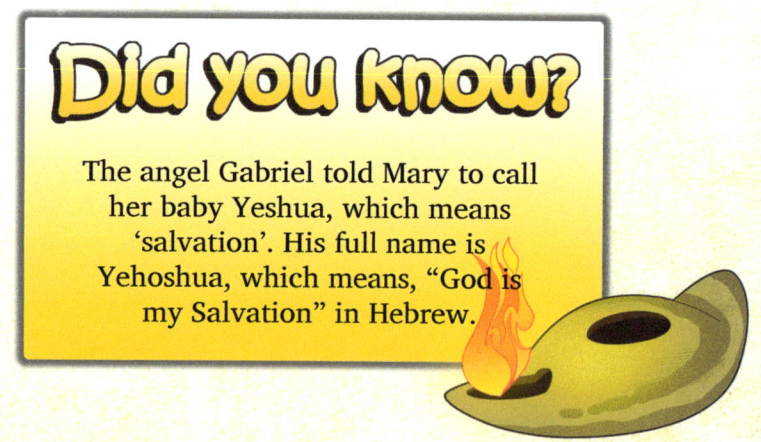

Did you know?

The angel Gabriel told Mary to call her baby Yeshua, which means 'salvation'. His full name is Yehoshua, which means, "God is my Salvation" in Hebrew.

Joseph was worried. Each night he tossed and turned in his bed. He wanted to do the right thing and take care of Mary, but what if that meant sending her away? Nazareth was a small town, and Joseph knew that news of Mary's baby would travel fast. He didn't want his neighbors talking badly about her. *"Maybe I should break off the engagement,"* he thought.

While Joseph thought about these things, an angel of God appeared to him in a dream. "Don't be afraid to take Mary home as your wife," said the angel. "The baby she will have was made by the Holy Spirit."

When Joseph woke up the next morning, he did what the angel had told him. He took Mary to be his wife. He was ready to trust God's plan.

Later that year, Caesar Augustus – the ruler of the powerful Roman Empire – ordered a census. The Romans ruled Judea and the Hebrews were forced to obey Rome's strict laws. Caesar wanted to know how many people he governed and how many he could tax. After all, there were lots of roads to build!

"Everyone must go back to his home town and register for the census," Caesar announced from his palace in Rome.

Because Joseph was a descendant of King David, he had to travel to Bethlehem, the town where David grew up. But Bethlehem was far away, and Mary needed to arrive before the baby was born. Joseph packed their bags, put Mary on a donkey, and set out for Bethlehem along a dusty dirt path.

Did you know?

The Romans worshipped a sun god called Sol Invictus (the unconquered sun). Every year they celebrated his birthday on December 25th.

After a long journey, Mary and Joseph finally reached the gate of Bethlehem. People welcomed them with open arms. "Shalom, shalom," they cried. "Barukh haba! Welcome!" Joseph knew God's Fall Appointed Times were about to start, and homes would soon be filled with guests. They needed to find a room fast. He trudged wearily through the crowded streets, looking for a place to stay.

Glowing oil lamps lit the homes of Bethlehem. Grey wisps of smoke curled high in the air. Soon Joseph found a place to stay. Because the upper room was full of people, Mary and Joseph were given space downstairs near the animals to sleep.

Mary rubbed her stomach and smiled. She was grateful for somewhere to stay. She sat in the courtyard, watching the women bake bread over the crackling fire. It was nearly the Day of Trumpets and the villagers had plenty to do. Mary could feel the excitement in the air.

Before long, Mary felt the baby kick inside her stomach. "The baby's coming!" she said anxiously to the women in the house. Mary had never had a baby before. She didn't know what to expect! The women crowded around, ready to help.

That night, the Messiah was born in Bethlehem. To keep the baby warm, Mary wrapped Him in linen cloth and placed Him carefully in an animals' manger filled with hay. She named him Yeshua, just as the angel had told her.

Joseph put his arm around Mary and gazed at the sleeping baby. "This baby is a gift from God," he said. They both knew this Child was very, very special.

Did you know?

The Day of Trumpets is one of God's Appointed Times. A shofar is blown 100 times and the last blast is known as the 'Last Trump'. This Appointed Time is when kings are announced or anointed.

In the hills around Bethlehem, a group of shepherds was guarding their sheep that night. Suddenly, an angel of God appeared above them with a flash! The shepherds covered their faces and stumbled backwards into the bushes. What was an angel doing here?

"Don't be afraid," said the angel. "I bring you good news, that will give everyone joy." The shepherds lay amongst the bushes and held their breath. They were too frightened to move or to even say a word!

"Today in Bethlehem, a baby was born who is the Messiah," said the angel. "You'll find Him wrapped in cloth and lying in a manger. Go and see Him."

All at once, the sky lit up with an army of angels praising God and singing, *"Glory to God! And on earth, peace and goodwill among the people!"*

The shepherds shook their heads in amazement. "Well, what are we waiting for?" they asked one another. "Let's go and see the Messiah!" They hurried to Bethlehem and found the place where Mary and Joseph were staying. The baby boy was fast asleep in a manger, just as the angel had told them.

Staring down at the sleeping baby, the shepherds said, "An angel appeared in the fields and told us this Child was the Messiah!" Everyone crowded around the shepherds and listened carefully. They had been waiting all their lives for a Messiah to rescue them from the Romans. Now He was finally here!

During this time, there was a powerful empire called the Parthian Empire. It was so big that it stretched from Persia all the way to the Indus River in the East. The Romans and Parthians didn't like each other much. They often sent their armies to fight each other.

Because the Parthian Empire was so big, the kings of Parthia had priests and nobles called Magi to help them make decisions. The Magi were important – they even helped choose the kings of Parthia! This is why they were called the "kingmakers."

The Magi were also astronomers. Every night, they studied the stars, waiting for a sign that the Messiah had arrived. They knew God had written His plan of salvation in the heavens. To ancient Hebrews, this was known as the Mazzaroth.

One evening, a great sign appeared in the sky. "It's finally arrived!" cried one of the Magi. He pointed excitedly to the night sky above them. More Magi rushed over to the window and peered up into the darkness. This was surely the sign that the prophet Balaam had spoken about in the Scriptures!

The Magi's hearts raced with excitement. "This means the Savior of Israel is here," they said, keeping their eyes glued to the heavens. They knew the Messiah's birth was important to people everywhere. "Let's go worship our newborn king!"

But the Magi would have to wait. Judea was far away and this would be a long and dangerous trip. They crowded together and began planning their great adventure.

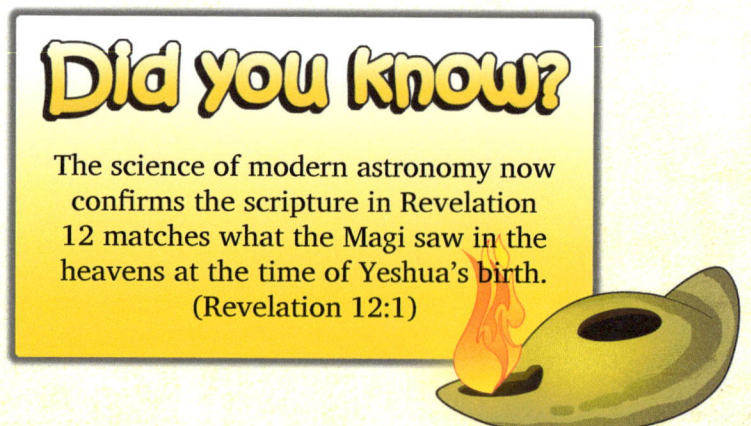

Did you know?

The science of modern astronomy now confirms the scripture in Revelation 12 matches what the Magi saw in the heavens at the time of Yeshua's birth. (Revelation 12:1)

Many months later, the Magi made their way along the stony roads toward Jerusalem. It was summer now and Judea was as hot as a giant furnace. Thieves roamed the countryside so the Magi were happy to have soldiers with them.

When the Magi reached Jerusalem, they made their way through the crowded city streets to the markets. "Where is the newborn King of the Jews?" they asked. "We saw His star from the East and have come to worship Him."

Crowds gathered in the alleyways and around the market stalls. "Who are the Parthians talking about?" they murmured uneasily. "Why have they come to Jerusalem?" Everyone knew the Parthians and Romans were fierce enemies.

Did you know?

The Wise Men (Magi) would have traveled approximately 900 miles to visit Yeshua. He was already a toddler by the time they reached Bethlehem.

At this time, King Herod was the ruler of Judea. He was furious to hear talk of a newborn king. "How dare these Magi ask for another king," he roared, slamming his fists on the table. "I am the king of the Jews!"

The Magi made King Herod nervous. Parthia was an enemy empire, and the Magi were important people. Caesar Augustus would not be pleased if he started another war. He summoned the chief priests and Torah teachers to his palace. "Where is this Messiah supposed to be born?" he asked them.

"The prophet Micah said a special king would be born in Bethlehem," they replied. They unrolled their Torah scrolls and showed him the Scriptures. It read: *"But you, Bethlehem, though you be little among the thousands of Judah, for from you shall come forth a ruler of My people, Israel."*

King Herod raised his hand to silence the priests. He had heard enough! "Go and fetch these Magi," he said. "Tell them to come and see me."

When the Magi arrived, Herod asked them, "When did this sign appear?" But the Magi knew King Herod was as cunning as a fox. They glanced at one another and answered carefully.

King Herod drummed his fingers on his throne. "Go and meet this newborn king," he said. He waved his hand towards Bethlehem. "Let me know when you find Him. I want to worship Him, too." But wicked King Herod didn't want to worship Yeshua; he wanted to kill Him. Herod believed he was the only king of the Jews!

Outside the palace, the Magi gazed up at the starry night sky. A bright star twinkled over Bethlehem, showing them the way. "Let's keep following this great sign!" they said, excitedly.

The Magi leaped on their horses and trotted through the city streets out into the open countryside. They could hardly wait to see the long-awaited Messiah.

Shepherds in the fields stared wide-eyed as the Magi passed by. "Why are the Parthians here?" they asked each another. The fierce-looking soldiers made them nervous. "Have they come to see the young boy, Yeshua?"

The Magi followed the star until it appeared over a house in Bethlehem where young Yeshua was staying. Leaping off their horses, they rushed inside to see Him. "Praise God; this is indeed the Messiah," they said.

The Magi fell to their knees and worshipped Yeshua with all their heart. Then with trembling hands, they opened their bags and handed him precious gifts of gold, frankincense, and myrrh.

But the Magi didn't stay long. God had warned them not to return to King Herod. Before he could find them, the Magi sped back to Parthia as fast as their horses could gallop.

Later that night, an angel of God appeared to Joseph in a dream. "Joseph, you are in great danger. Get up, and take your family to Egypt. Stay there until I tell you to leave. Herod wants to kill the Child."

Joseph shook Mary gently. "Wake up," he whispered. "We must escape before King Herod finds us and kills Yeshua. God wants us to go to Egypt." Mary nodded, but her stomach felt tight. What had God planned this time?

Quickly they packed up their bags and slipped out of the house, onto the streets of Bethlehem. Somewhere a dog barked. The town was dark and empty. Egypt was far away, but Mary and Joseph knew God would take care of them.

Did you know?

King Herod was of Arab descent, not Jewish. Even though he was called the king of Judea, he was given this title by Rome, not the Israelites.

When King Herod heard the Magi were gone, he was as mad as a firecracker. He paced back and forth, shaking his fists. "How dare the Magi go back to Parthia!" he thundered. "I've been tricked!"

Herod called for his officers. "Go to Bethlehem and kill all the boys under two years old," he said. "Destroy this so-called king. I want him gone!"

But it was too late. Mary and Joseph had already left for Egypt with the Child. It would be a while before they saw their homeland again, but Yeshua was safe. Little did they know that this was all part of God's wonderful plan to restore His people back to the House of Israel.

THE END

TEST YOUR KNOWLEDGE!
(Match the question with the answer at the bottom of the page)

QUESTIONS

What name did Gabriel tell Mary to call her son? ....

Who ordered a census of the Roman world? ....

Why did Mary and Joseph travel to Bethlehem for the census? ....

In which town was Yeshua born? ....

Who was king of Judea at this time? ....

Who did angels appear to in the fields? ....

In which place did the prophet Micah say the Messiah would be born? ....

How many magi (Wise Men) visited Yeshua after He was born? ....

What did King Herod do after the Magi tricked him? ....

To which land did Joseph, Mary, and Yeshua flee? ....

ANSWERS

1. Yeshua
2. Emperor Augustus
3. They were descendants of David from Bethlehem
4. Bethlehem
5. Herod (the great)
6. Shepherds
7. Bethlehem
8. The Bible doesn't say
9. Gave orders to kill every boy in Bethlehem under two years old
10. The land of Egypt

Complete the Word Search Puzzle

MANGER NAZARETH
JOSEPH MARY
HEROD   MESSIAH
ANGEL   MAGI
BETHLEHEM SHEPHERDS

```
B J O S E P H M M S
H E X N M O H E A H
P E T C O A J S R E
E Y R H E Z G S Y P
A N E O L F L I O H
J U O Y D E K A O E
V X L P A E H H Z R
A N G E L A Y E M D
N A Z A R E T H M S
Z A W M A N G E R Y
```

Bible Pathway Adventures®

Betrayal of the King
The Risen King
Swallowed by a Fish
The Chosen Bride
Saved by a Donkey
Thrown to the Lions
Facing the Giant
Samson Mighty Warrior
Sold into Slavery
The Great Flood
Shipwrecked!
The Exodus
Escape from Egypt

Discover more Bible Pathway Adventures' Bible stories!

Check out Bible Pathway Adventures' Activity Books

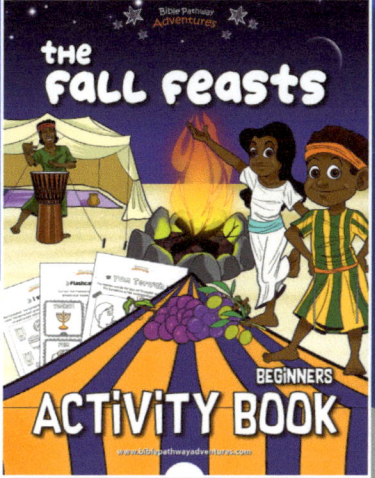
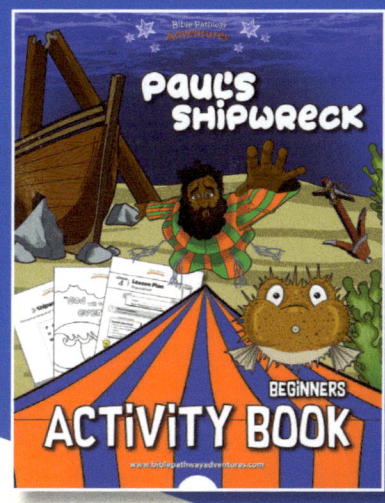

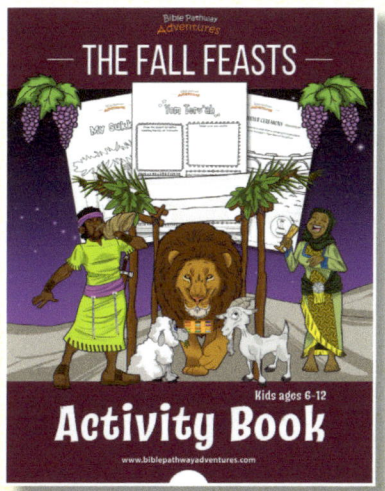

GO TO

www.biblepathwayadventures.com